MW01265105

# RHYME BOOK

How to write a Rap song :

1. Brainstorm.
2. Create a Hook.
3. Write lyrics.
4. Be personal.
5. Organize.
6. Memorize.
7. Rap and share.

This Book belong to :